MARY MAGDALENE POEMS

Margaret A. Harrell

ISBN (hardcover): 979-8-9904800-8-7
ISBN (pbk): 979-8-9904800-9-4
ISBN (audio): 979-8-9931240-2-5
ISBN (audio): 979-8-9931240-5-6

Part Four of *Mary Magdalene Poems* was previously published in *Particle Piñata Poems*.

A Published in Heaven Series Book
Published in Heaven Books include titles by His Holiness
The Dalai Lama, President Jimmy Carter, Thomas
Merton, Seamus Heaney, Hunter S. Thompson, Jack
Kerouac, Andy Warhol, Allen Ginsberg, Yoko Ono, William
S. Burroughs, Edvard Munch, Diane di Prima, Jim Carroll,
Amiri Baraka, Gregory Corso, John Updike, Rita Dove,
Wendell Berry, David Amram, Douglas Brinkley, BONO,
Ron Whitehead, Lawrence Ferlinghetti, and many more.
Published in conjunction with Saeculum University Press of
Sibiu, Romania, and Raleigh, North Carolina

For inquiries, signed copies, and speaking requests, contact
the author. at margaretharrell.com

A goose's quill has put an end to murder
That put an end to talk

—Dylan Thomas

How *I* Predicted
Me
And you can too

---My whole life has been
A Prediction I Made

CONTENTS

PRELUDE

Had I never made it,
What would have happened?
Where would "I," the one here now,
be
Lost in the never-had-been?
Or just in the "waiting room?
Or even patient as a
guide over my head
But that didn't happen
Let me tell you what did
It's instructive
It's what you can choose to do
too

Predict you

Which I did over and over,
guided myself to myself
without knowing I was doing it
in the blankness of wondering who I was
Who am I? you ask and then
You can choose to

Predict you

Just like Nostradamos
Or any prognosticator
taking out the crystal ball
reaching out across distances

But the thing is, this kind of prediction works in—

I know

trying to reach me
show
anyone who has a yen to

Anyone?
Yes, exactly
how easy it is to begin
their predictions
too

how it works?
Yes, exactly
Adding in all the tech tools, though even in the past,
sitting with quill in hand, you could be, without
knowing it,
Predicting
You

without knowing it
using writing tools, acting tools, and so forth to
connect with that possibility of YOU
conscious, even
Waiting in Being,
In Becoming
Waiting for you to
Predict the existence of
the reality calling
to

you

OK, we've got that established
There's a technique not taught to us whereby
Imagining we're imagining, we're actually in an inner
spaceship
en route to the grand discovery of

The me I
Made up

But this is very serious stuff
Highly serious
Even top secret
And just like that it's released upon the Earth

Yes, to any and all who can
Take seriously
The me I made up

Waiting for you to
in invisibility
didn't become
Pick out
craft, concoct, listen to
the reality calling you to

think, in the blanks and sightlessness, the
unidentified future
you sitting on
the sidelines

You mean I sidelined myself?

Everybody does it
Imagine calling yourself out onto the field

when you've been
in the dugout

out of the game

No one suspecting you were an instigator
come down from
a different dimension

A waste, I'd say
to spend a lifetime with no idea of that option

We all do it
I did it
Stop it
Call in your true Self

So you predicted yourself

I just took a look and said, *There's got to be more to
it.*

You mean, more to you?

Yes, I said: *I don't believe this is all there is to me.*

And then what?

Support flew in
Inexplicable forms of entities and beings

That were you?

there to lend a hand to me

To me too?

To you too

Writing indentations into the paper
of my future
scratching indentations into the paper
into the atmosphere
pressing thoughts into actions because of
—attraction
—"bringing"
 me in

Untying the knots, the
refusals
in my head
so easy to do
on paper
only paper, I thought

Say what comes into
your head

setting up
acquiescence
momentum

Telling me, dictating, as to William Blake
whose dictation
"brought"
him in
Would there have been a Blake without his
early morning
5 a.m.
talking to spirits,

convocations of them
up to listen to them
dictate
—so he said
taking down poems
To

"bring"
William Blake in

But what of others
Writing themselves into
Existence

Earth history
as themselves
and not
a pretender
for they were really scribes of their own
Existence
Writing
themselves
In

Thoughts clinging in the air
all about
pressed into our reality but in fact

called into service to create
these bunches of
Energies
Attracting to them
Everything they needed to
Be
Down Here

come in style
Be in their own skin, their thoughts surrounding
them like a sheltering
tent and bedding
their histories condensed there
Gathered-up potential left over from "last time"

Or "never came here, but went there"
or just "never was, am now"
Our forefathers at their backs with thoughts
that swirled into a materialized shape
Here now in an incarnation

these carriers of
Our options for
today

Every time you feel your fingers lift to write
What do you think is lifting
the cloak we're *sitting under*
Vis-à-vis you

Well. I liked that answer
It gave me some assurance, as
I hadn't a clue what I was to write next
I sat in concentration, in absorption, in
disappearance,
my head screwed into tight focus, staring at the page
Were more words going to pop out onto it,
materialize at the behest of
my typing fingers?
I hadn't a clue.
My brain didn't know

I didn't even know if this was part of the other book I
just started

Over here there's a giant spurt
But over here, *don't miss this one*
Back over there
How can I keep it up?
Again, is this the same book?
pouring out of that faucet?

Think again

I guess Awareness just woke up from a long slumber

Or you stumbled onto it

OK
Now that we've received this invitation,
Not just to writers, thinkers, to anyone receiving bits
and pieces of themselves
Barely given the time of day
That are really their most neglected, elusive
opportunities come to give them the Stage, the
spotlight, of their
So-called
higher self
Tell us
what do we do to
emulate—

Me? Heaven forbid
To emulate yourself
The one who knows all this
who's

I know
waiting

PREAMBLE

Predict Your Life

You Can, You Know

How I Discovered
Me by Predicting Me

Somewhere I existed
I put out the call, Come

PART ONE

Lights Dimmed
In the dark about our life

What's this all about? You put out the call *come*
That doesn't make sense
There you were
How could you *predict* you'd be alive?
Isn't that backwards?

No,
Think of yourself as steps
A ladder
You're on one rung
You can't see above you, accessible if you just
Say

I know
You said,
"Come"

As the cloud of particles swirled
just thoughts swooping into my head
Caught excitedly
Alive, happy to be in somebody's head, I thought
I wrote it, "received" the future
Unknown to me
And so that became me
That's how I became

A prediction I made

Would you have been that you if you had not cared
to catch them
caught the thoughts?

What an idea—that ideas form us

That consciousness comes first?
That consciousness comes first

Yes, let me explain
In my case, I was writing ideas I didn't understand
Thinking my inspiration did
It gave them to me
So how exciting to put them down
But in fact it was me all along
The me I was calling in
Or that was

Yes

Pulling you as on a rope to it
The self who wanted to exist and depended on you
To hold on to what it knew but you didn't
Not yet
Till it got to you and opened
that aspect of you, making you exist

What a thought
Well, say, it was in terms of levels and combinations
of potential
So I said come and

—yes, that level of your potential had been waiting for
that moment

had you not been bored with the reality you were in
wanting to go to the next edge of being
you would never have gotten there
not by reading
not by thinking

So I listened myself here

Yes, you listened to the echo when you said

I said

Come

Consciousness swam ahead and I followed
filled with its

Its what?

with my-
self

Exactly.
Now, you're finally on to something
Now you know how it works
Up there where thoughts
think
And you were a thought that

Thunk you up.

Higher beings don't work like that

Who thought who up?
What are you talking about?"

"Put your doubts aside and listen
It's what you're used to doing
Bear with me

If you'll clarify one thing
are you

God?

"The God in you."

OK. Keep on.
So I am a Creator
I created me
I'm not having any of it
It's too lonely
No fun
Scary as all get-out

So this gave me second thoughts
I mean the screen savers on my computer and such
I thought it was miscoloring the true colors of the
world
But wait a minute
Colors are vibrations
Who reads them better?
Lots to take pause over
Lots to bout around
think twice
about

First thing waking up, what do I do?

I say, *What do you want to do, Day?*
If you are lonely, try it
Imagine the Day is there
Wanting to be—?
fulfilled, of course
Wants to be
not just spilled out into data in a huge AI program

Try it
Step in

Well, you'll never know if you don't try to make
contact

Like to a UFO?
Exactly

Talk to the Day
Ask it if it's sitting there
perhaps on your bed
Or more abstractly
in the air around you
Sitting there in options it can present to you
in the now of that minute as you look for it
Ask it if it's there
And what it has
in store for you
If you just
Ask for it
look for it

The Awareness in
The day

Never will I forget walking inside a consciousness—
not mine—

A solemnity, a compactness of focus, it's hard to
describe
as if inside Sensing itself
So then, I was inside a consciousness—not mine, that
was clear
I didn't know whose consciousness—
just found myself in its <u>location</u>. In no-time?
No Place? Walking slowly, repeatedly, seeming to
move without moving, going somewhere without
getting anywhere.

it had been
I later figured out, a practice session,
The great guru taking that walk, in Dhyanyogi-ji's
case, those months
before "dropping the body"
he walked and walked inside a smoky gray path
I was inside
his consciousness. I figured it out.

For him, it was to end in—?
the universe
Maha Samadhi
Like diving from the very tip end of a diving board
into the great sea of consciousness

But what about you, Margaret?

End of the long walk through darkness
What
Waited For You
There?

Welcome
babies
crying out to *know*
hanging in hammocks
of it
information
welcomed in
hammocks of
your
consciousness

surrounded by events of You
rocking in
events of You
hammocks holding
You
in your
consciousness

But surely he knew how to meet death
he didn't need to rehearse
So suppose it wasn't just death at the end of that long
walk, I finally asked

as the implications took decades to unfold
Of course, he wasn't just walking the plank to death
That was old stuff to him
He was walking
a path for the Earth
with the Earth

creating a path that would exist,
bright though it looked like utter darkness
as he bored, with his focus, ahead
But without panic
Without Knowing but walking with Knowing at his
side
Finding
a breakthrough
Either soon or centuries after
any single person and the Earth could later track
Walking an attitude
to carry in our exploring
The way through the tunnel of
What Might be Next

"All his life," I heard, "Milton measured his days in—
—coffee spoons, did you say?

—in waste

—Not to be "allowed to"
do what he was primed to
a sign said: "Don't go there!"
Ah, a viable life plan
Not to be.

Yes, a pattern
To—?
Overturn

Knock the pattern
for a loop as friends stared in—

Consternation?

Yes, why wasn't he famous?
Why didn't he give the <u>signal</u> to them to *"begin"*

—of course
let's just
Spout the gift out in conversation
Speak those poem lines
Those kernels of tightly condensed philosophy
Those word tools
Not to be recorded
By him, that is

Oh, but you recorded them

Some, yes

But suppose
He gave it to

you?

The mind, the spirit,
the physical relics of it, its creations
Wafted into the breezes
from the mouth
A talker

But this is not an oral century.
Oops
What? wrong notch on the dial

Just don't let him
Turn on the
Creative writing juices

"They're waiting for *me*," he told me,
his friends were
expected him to give the signal to begin
But he never gave it
raced out of the gate in a <u>signal</u> that all of them were
to come out at once

Agonized, his Earth self not in on the plan
down here in his Earth self
that wasn't the plan at all

But look!

I received a signal
Was it him on some higher plane of reality
—that beggar desperate for a
—yes, telltale cigarette
the cigarette hanging out of Milton's mouth
who wrote of God that he would
No, surely God has nothing to do with cigarettes
—wrote that God would
light our cigarette
with his

But couldn't the beggar you saw at Montparnasse have
just begged for money?

No, a cigarette would help me recognize him
Just five months later when I—

    I know, you walked into the Corner Bistro and
    Saw his eyes gleaming in the dark, smoke-filled
            corner, eyes just like

            I know
            Rimbaud's

      As if you'd never left

            I know
            Pari

    I think you're typing up loose ends now

Don't you think it's time to?

Watch for our prompts

PART
TWO

Take your hammer
Take your chisel
Take your instruments
And do not fizzle this
Come, child
Come, adult
As you were, soldier
Come to this story's present incidents and
settings

You scattered yourself to the many winds. In the physical this means that you have divided up your lessons so that none are kept for you. The precious gift of learning has not been seen as a gift by you, as a sense of gathering and harvesting. So you must gently go back to each position where you gave someone a piece of your path. How can you walk on a path that you didn't allow the pieces to lay themselves down on?

—Seth

Yogi gesticulated to talk. As I remained silent, He expounded, "Balkumar, once a person came to Bhagawan Ramana and said something similar to this: 'Everyone in this ashram is working and doing jobs. You alone are sitting simply without doing any work. Why don't you do something like others?" Bhagawan Ramana retorted: "THERE IS NO OTHERS!" . . .

Birds, trees, animals, plants, stone, mud, sea, sky, wind, humans—nothing is separate. Everything is One. That's called God. You and I are part of Him. You are in me, and I'm in you. In an ocean, is there a difference in the waves? Are two sea waves different? . . . Within ocean, they may separate themselves as waves and bubbles. But . . . Each wave and each bubble are part of the whole sea; rising and dissolving are an appearance. In fact, they are not different from the ocean. And so are we, like the sea waves in the ocean.[a]

PART THREE

LARGER MEASURES.
YARDSTICKS with centuries on them
Sent
from a Timeless realm
Found later in different rooms, different files
defragmented
behold
nevertheless,
they fit

But then a voice said
"Once you were a hero

Je sais ouvrir
La bout-
eille."

*"I know how to open
the bottle."*

Dig here, Earth

the
Mot

Not the *moi, idiot?*[1]
No, not the *me*

the mot
the Word
Am-

mot

---

[1] *mot*: "word" (FR). pronounced "mo"; *moi*: "me" (FR)

Rolling the double ten
Let there be light

IN
Light
Ten

My mother was going to die
Did she know the car was to crash into her?

she left me, carefully crafted
No envelope—
three words
mailed it through friends
as safe as by carrier pigeon
surer than any post

I had driven my brand-new used Chevy to
Charlottesville, my new home
let her know, "I got here."
What did she do?
Well, nothing?
No, then—one of her friends
—at the after-burial reception
relayed back to me
—she, one by one, phoned her friends to give them
the news:
this squirreled-away message safely delivered
"She made it"

my mother left it to me,
that prediction that—

Did you say prediction?
Yes, she predicted
how my life would turn out
through all the topsy-turvy challenges
Never to lose sight of
gauging from this little instance
she sent back to me—struck by a car
wouldn't be there to see it, but
the miniature model giving her the chance—

predicted
that—in the Big Drive Home
of my Indy 500 or was it Daytona
racetrack life

recorded into the Universe's ear
that—
I—

she pressed on the horn, shouted—beeped it
—from the heavens, from the housetops
—"made it"

She predicted it?

She predicted it
No doubt about it
None whatsoever

that the last time she saw me, getting into that
secondhand car,
foreshadowed the Drive of the Rest of My Life
And that helping me buy that car
insisting on repairing the horn
she participated too
Set me out on a winning streak
in the Drive Home
by way of The Rest of My Life

It was that important, was it?

Yes, in the next stop, Zurich Jung Institute,
there it was on the map;
Hornwweg

I kept the words close,
How she told all her **friends, one by one,**

"she"—I—"made it."

I wish I knew WHO I was talking to

*A divine being, but I haven't a clue. To
me you are just Friend, Being, who
comes to talk to me, sit with me."*

*Isn't that enough? I never use a name.
How about From the Source. Won't
that do for identification?*

Well, no, actually. I would love a name.

*Well, will Nameless do?
Nameless is what I'm using right now
for this book.
I'm going to call you Spot On*

Couldn't be truer

PART FOUR

Messages to the Earth
Guides, Initiations, Word Play
In Partnership with the Spirit World

This collection of writings, going back to 1985, was in the energies working tirelessly to see long-sightedly and specifically into the twenty-first century. Predictive, seeing ahead. Consciousness whispering even then that change was afoot. Carrying this baton. Relevant, even more so now.

The whole odyssey first signaling its existence at the Dôme Café, a few blocks from the Cimetière du Montparnasse, in Paris, where the young poet Charles Baudelaire, in 1867, just forty-six years old, was buried. Likewise, Man Ray, Simone Beauvoir, Sartre, and Samuel Beckett had their afterlife homes there.

Consider what you have in the smallest chosen library. A company of the wisest and wittiest men that could be picked out of all civil countries in a thousand years have set in best order the results of their learning and wisdom.

The men themselves were hid and inaccessible, solitary, impatient of interruption, fenced by etiquette; but the thought which they did not uncover to their bosom friend is here written out in transparent words to us, the strangers of another age.

—Ralph Waldo Emerson

I become a transparent eye-ball; I am nothing; I see all; the currents of the Universal Being circulate through me; I am part and parcel of God.

—Walt Whitman

Opening Salvo

What? That spot of dust over there
That leaf on a tree
That sentence that spouted out of someone's
mouth
That color red put on by a person when I
wore red
Were "my" ideas appearing out there
somewhere else?
So how to do it?
How to establish that
Yes, I am
One with God and God is
One with You

1

Encounters with Milton Klonsky after his death

From the nothingness of thin air

My *Experience—no, vision*—of Reality

In meditation I saw
Milton Klonsky, now a spirit guide
a sudden looming apparition of himself pointed me
to a spinning form
—I instantly knew what it was—
Dazzling, dangled in front of me,
A vision of "the Whole," the All—
Consciousness Itself

As if he made a scaled model of it

I watched in instant understanding
As he stepped out of flesh and blood into this
meditation room
as if it were easy to make the transition
Appearing in my mind, my eyes shut,
Plucking essence from a Tree of Understanding
As if held out in his hand, Here it is
Satori

I saw

information moving as
a whole—it could not do otherwise, its nature
seemingly—
bound together but not tightly;
shifting,
as it rippled through the All—
the fabric of it
precipitated by a
single insertion of movement—from anywhere—a
single new fact

What in quantum mechanics language we deemed
irreversible

As options in the "cloud of possibility" in the particle
realm
collapsed
and a unique event in time emerged—
was, to the whole,
the non-stand-still Unity,
recoverable.
It reorganized, in instant information-aware pieces
inherent meaning kept moving, "processed"
instantly—
acknowledged
in less than a split second juxtapositions
call it the
quantum jumps of "information
units"
"position-aware"
 Feedback
or resonating
Reshufflings.

Shift after shift,
Registered
Realigning,
—transcendent consciousness
that did not have to "think," merely to contain
Self-arranging, self-attracting information bits that
excluded nothing
Aware of every move

now one, *now another* point, a new angle, *energized
by the whole.*

We screeched to a halt to invest in our reality as it
cemented itself to us; feeling it definitive, made
concrete.

But every single
perspective/point/information bit that existed, even
potentially, could have *all information
brought to bear
if its turn came
AND it* in turn *came forward*
—acting on *its* information,
its experience.

I watched as if looking at a UFO the All's nonstop
spinning
recalibrating with new information, absorbing
digesting it
in a nano-instant encompassing the ramifications in
all directions of *any additional fact
or event, reinforcing Whichever centers of*

captured attention
now—

it is unpredictable to us what event the wave function
will favor in the cloud of congregating particles
the selection process is not up to
the particles (we think)
the "cloud" breaks
and one raindrop falls into, overtakes
our reality

But here I "saw"
a veil removed so I could watch
Satori
that every new fact, event, bit of information spins
with the All, in the whole
as in a Vegas casino wheel,
without thought, without hesitation, "time"

When we observe and collapse something—our
"life"—out of countless choices
the Whole absorbs that shift, that new status *of itself*
And spins on, now different,
though with no discernible "stop."

In the perspective of the "whole," I saw—
the collapse is only
of "information." As if to a
non-time-bound level of Consciousness the outcome
in our 3-D world was a thought puzzle (*that could be
rethought*).
Nothing was ever at a standstill there.

Anything in our matter world could regroup, reboot, wait for its turn again, or leap into the new Now

I wondered, who/what was conscious
In this motion so fast
so "unthinking,"
or rather a kaleidoscope of invisible "thought"
become instant knowledge,
understanding, by association

I did not see the individual awareness
Just Awareness itself
Consciousness itself
Attached to no Aware-er per see
All
Aware
My delight, my joy, my astonishment

Measurement Poems

A Communiqué

from my old mentor, Milton, a terse message out of
"nowhere," again in the nothingness of thin air

Starkly advising:

"*Measure Me*"

—proffering the suggestion
perplexingly
*—dangling the mere idea—that his own energy (perish
the thought) could be measured*

*Or asking me to tackle that conundrum of whether it
could*

He sent it telepathically:
*Look, here's a good assignment. Look, I don't
need to spell it out. You see what I mean.*

Okay. So you like to
Use a random number generator in your apartment.
(Very much so.) But look.

I'm not here, physically speaking.
Were far from my Greenwich Village room
My bird nest aerie
Yet wouldn't you agree I'm very much here?
I challenge you, try to take a
measurement of
my size, my dimensions.
My presence, location, speed,

my composite interactions.

The message popped in
on my mental screen, a screen
that didn't exist either.

As I stood in nature with my Belgian light body teacher
in Ibiza, "journeying" in meditation
And suddenly my soul grouping "appeared" in my
mind's eye in a U shape open ended
And Milton broke rank, stepping forth
With the question

I instantly saw the irony
I examined it up close, spellbound,
—turned it around—
To form yet another question.
Well, hmmm,

What if I measure *myself*

Look, *So here's a conundrum.*
"Can you—? Just envision it

But wasn't I thinking small?

The thought expanded

What if I measure *myself?*

Round the coastline of me several times over,
skidding and falling to the ground and getting back
up and looking around
walking, taking the compass out, and the ruler, and the
yardstick, and the markers,
and whatnots, and finding that
this coastline of myself is irregular and also
furthermore
it is shifting as I walk through it
asking how to

MEASURE MYSELF

which locations *and which ways* a not
continually, not exclusively
physical—well, you see how to get the hang of it.

Earlier, in a physical body, Milton had assigned me a
different project, remembering his own failings:
 "Don't let *time* measure *you. You*
measure it."

Another measuring rod

But wasn't this harder? The simple task, given from
outer space—
real, warm, heart-challenging—

"Measure *me.*"

Of course, you, I, everyone had this task
not of finding out
who they are, but the implication would
exist—
that you were the one *there* and *there*
in my kitchen as I brush garlic on steak
but what about over there as you sleep
he had also once stated the principle to me
of space, time, AND PLOT,
How could there be a space-time dimension
without plot?
So hold on, now. See what it turns into. Like a
measuring
rod into personality, soul "size," presence,
energetic survival.
Not Planck lengths but the length of connections

It implied: well, look, if the length of a fractal is
infinite, what about me?
as the threads wore thin or
strengthened.
Into—?

take my weight, that's easy
take my height and—well, let's not say depth—

take my width,
but suppose you ask instead
to find the boundaries of—
myself

my Plot-located energy?

Measure with the RNG?
Fine and well

But while at it . . .
I flipped open the trans-dimensional cell phone
How do you measure a huge energy
Even a tiny energy, personified,
Calling it
"me"?

2

Gâteau Poems[2]
For the Earth, a "Cook-Key"

Baudelaire's prose poem "Le Gateau" ("The Cake")"
started me off on this roller coaster,
Wham-bam
particles collided
chasing transformations as the "cake" revealed itself
to be a planetary "cook-key," cooking up—?
for the Earth
the beginning of the twenty-first century

All hands on deck!
here's a
Cook-Key
The syllables hit Attraction points
Wham-Bam
From The Christ State
A language mix-up
a
Cook-Key

---

[2] *gâteau*—cake, pronounced "got tow"; *eau* is pronounced "O";
all French here and below

A Coin Flip

a Tour de Force
dangerous, daring plan

crossing language barriers

That should make a good setting
In the stratospheres of
syllables at play

Was the *Last Supper*
A
Commedía
in mid-syllable, a language shift

secret relationships—two, three languages—sliding in,
safe, on base

comer—to eat—in Spanish
co-*mère*[3]
spinning, dashing into each other,
what do you get?
A *comer* (to eat) Dia

---

[3] *mère*—mother (Fr); *día*—day (Sp and Pt); co-may-día: *Divina*
Commedia—Divine Comedy

Commedia.

Dante comes in: Hmmmmm. Perfect for the twenty-
first century Let's call in Baudelaire.
Bringing
a nice *gâteau*
birthday cake
Hmmm.
Now, everyone remember, bring your best gift for the
new century,
your most cherished
In donation to humanity
In donation to its unity, its Ground, its common
Love
Lift Off

The Meta-4

So if we see the world as a Thought Form
the fourth dimension is a
meta4
the oven where the cooking, the cake, was timed a
FOUR⁴[foo-ur]
Hold on now
A (French) four [foo-ur] is . . . ?

an (English) OVEN

A Cook-Key
ready to come out in the open

a GOT TOW

Now what could be cooking
in a *meta*
Four. Turned On High
*En Haut*⁵
["O" – h-a-ut – is "high" in French]

Turned On High

_____

⁴ *four*—oven, pronounced "foo-er"
⁵ *en haut*—on high; *haut is* pronounced "O" (*eau:* water, also
pronounced "O")

En Haut
in O
the *haut* in the end
not N-O now
En Haut

A turned around spelling coming in
in

a
Meta-4

II

Ready to go, then
a New Era
here to Fore

God not
in the No anymore
The Littlest Plot
given volition

the most tiny
the wee Ours

Can we Trump-et an ending out of this?

For the Earth to go to a higher state
the karma had to be absorbed—
the lesson reversed

On one side he would be
of *the fenêtre*, window
hourglass

the signal *Now*: yes

for there was that certitude the *fenêtre* was
an *our*
glass

A Tour Nay
to turn no into yes
a courtship battle
in a
Tour
Nay

And now we learn the formula that will unbind
this web

Hologram Rhet finally
gotten beyond
as we go on with
Emily Brontë
out of
D-Quai

Is humankind ready then for this new turn?
—to step into the twenty-first century
and what is being stepped into?
—does it appear to be governed by?
High Comedy

an old signal
in the universe activated, to sense
sentir[6]

III

We on the Earth located our exploration outside
This project—located inside—was
digging into
the true nature
of Man
in crisis position
where only one could survive
which one was the true one?
The Ego representative—
did that represent humankind?

Surely not—

A love that through centuries had been dwarfed
by the transcendent spirit
now the transcendent spirit
put all the strength behind the heart

In Terror gate
to ask of your Self in terror
in Terror
Gate
who am I?
Then do it

---

[6] *sentir*—to feel

go through it
GATE O[7]
Once there was a woman who had two beautiful
cookies
she put them under a spell and said
whatever happens
gâteaux say no

Got toe will travel

Got
toe
say
no

It must have something to do with a gate
Keeping him away from
a gate
—A Gate O
The *gâteaux*
who said no

And then someone said:
Take 2
GOT 2

At the reins
riding into the arena
In

------

[7] Gate O—a twist on *gâteau*, got tow; *eau:* water (also
pronounced "O")

formation

a chariot-
Tier

Ali-
Gate
Tor
GATE TOW
GATE-A Ω

IV

Will you marry me? asked the *oui* cell?
What? Marry the *oui*[8]
cell

He wanted
his Rites
demanded
she must give him
His Rites

The story that had never been told
The love story that had never been told
that slowly it can be told
the story of Jesus and
Mary Magdalene

----

[8] *oui*—yes; pronounced "we"

and so he threw her thoughts into faraway orbit,
where
they seemed to be having—if thoughts could have
them—a fling
like the fastest birds, the swifts, who mate in the air
and throw themselves off a cliff or a nest,
these thoughts, as if they were javelins being
thrown,
as far as the mightiest thrower could, seemed to be
having if thoughts could be said to
something like a fling.
In the depths of the archetype
there is almost no way
to deal with it
and an archetype one has oneself lived in
repeatedly

There was only emotion to deal with
massive amounts of emotion
accumulation
of emotion from over centuries
the whole treasure in it
the heart trans-
Plantation

Not to run
Not to run

this time
not to

V

In all those stories
what never got told
The seashell never
picked up
the one never heard sing
the one where the love story made its expression

the song sung now by
his soul
Nep-
TUNE

To plug into the energy of Jesus at a point where
something had never been said—
the seashell never picked up

the *Oui* Cell

The Littlest Plot
now we begin
to lift the lid

Mary Magdalene

I know how I was born
what I came out of
I was the spark that wouldn't
that couldn't
go out

I wouldn't go out to be born
Yet neither would I
Nor COULD I
go out

The love story filled all the bookshelves
It entered all the libraries
of the spark that wouldn't
THAT couldn't go out

Embedding itself in the history of very intelligent
men
having followed their brains
who buried their hearts

A Sublet

All this a secret enactment on the astral plane
all this totally unknown to the Earth
as the Exit of the Old Man began
as he with his helicopter tied around the Earth drew
it to the next Stage
But his own story—that there underneath at the
bottom deepest in his heart
the one that began
When Jesus looked down from the Cross
what dream was in his heart
Was it the New Year's Eve we did the town
Was it the one coming up on his horizon
Was it the one he forgot about
Was it that dream?
Did he
reserve that dream
in his heart where no one would ever see it
till the negative was clearly finished
and the light ready to come on
to be turned on
how it developed in the dark through centuries
And this is it
the new development on that plot
that Jesus looking down on the Cross thought of
and got sustenance from
his love for
Mary Magdalene
D
I
D

The Old Man's Right to Privacy in His Own FIRE-side

I didn't know that holding so firmly to my reins of
the Truth
for myself I would wind up in this unconscious
energy of the
Earth and all the things people never said
that would have made history go another way
I had no idea that if I did it well enough
if my heart was blown wide open
and my mind blown wide open
but in the end my heart
so that nothing else mattered
I would wind up in the Alternative Revelation
so deep it took centuries of master-hearting to get to
it
a 2,000-year PLOT
by the boldest minds imaginable
but they found their hearts all this time
in being master minds
had got omitted

And they'd had that style of it enough
they would say their message from the heart
well, just look what the real answer was
practically saying there will be no 21st century
if the King stepped down
dethroned himself
for what was that crown
if he couldn't share
couldn't have a heart like other men

In lesson form
the lessons they had learned
HIS HAND
THE OLD MAN'S
when he reveals it

As he's opening my hand now
the hand I didn't know I had
that I was one of those who agreed and even shouted
that I
wanted to do this
help bring in the Real RITES OF MAN
starting with the rites of his own FIRE SIDE
the Old Man's privacy in his own FIRE SIDE
he had never been allowed that
because where could he get protection enough
it didn't exist
how to protect
A VIBRATION LIKE THIS
his own when he looked at Mary Magdalene
just as he had on the Cross
and then he'd get strength from her

My computer when I felt the question and wrote it
wrote the
answer
as the power behind it is fueling everything written
here

D
I
D

Lessons for the Earth in its changing position
now what use for a
medium
THE MEDIUM
OF
LOVE

LOVE
IN
TRANSITION
THE MEDIUM
Of LOVE

For it was in the air now
the germ of it all
the real story behind
The American Dream
in this version
The real one
A
MARY
CAN

As entities had moved into the orbit of the Earth
to bring to the Earth
in transformation stories they themselves and others
had made
lessons for the Earth in its changing position
now what use for a medium:
the Medium
OF LOVE

Love in Transition
in the medium of Love

Atelier Dante

The Earth barreling into the twenty-first century,
with most of the inhabitants unaware of the
challenges it would face—
raced toward

[longer pause]
At the computer
COMMAND
DANTE

Watching the screen
cheering us on
a TELLY YAY[9]
a Telly Yay

A desire to vacuum the Earth
to restore its beauty
to value what had seemed insignificant
had no place
the idea penetrating
that without this sense of nature
life was not worth living
more it would disappear

This a message from the future
just as Robert had received a message

---

[9] An *atelier*, or workshop (FR), is roughly pronounced "a telly yah"

from his future self
telling him to
self-destruct
telling now the inhabitants of the Earth
to self-destruct
from their present path
get off that path

To the Earth
I

Extra, extra, read all about it—
the End of the World
everywhere, alarms were going off,
people waking up
waiting for this signal
the end of the world
waiting to bring it about
the end of the world

Robert died.
It was the end of the world.

People waking up
inner alarms going off
rung from the astral plane
A man on the astral plane
clanging the dinner bell
saying there was food for the masses
come to the gathering
meet here to dine
That the food long in preparation was ready
that there was sole for breakfast
As in the biblical days
make from one fish food for everyone
For the New Age breakfast was ready
And the breakfast of the New Age
was the sole of Man

The breakfast of the New Age was being prepared
Now everything fell into place

people waking up
understanding the inner ringing
Hearing it in their sleep
from a clock
that was invisible
Audible this sound
from high up in the astral plane
calling Man to wake up
that a truck was driving to his/her door this very
minute
a delivery being made
a green truck
a spring truck
it was
under way
the leap into the New Age

Outwardly a chaotic scene
a world out of control
but inwardly
the chance of ages
the buildup of thousands of years
for the outer disturbance
is a mirror
from across a window
a window into Man's soul
and in that soul the end of the world is a blessing
an age is being carried out.
People waking up
inner alarm ringing
ringing in
the New Age
And then the overall structure became clear

there was clarity
there was a plot behind the apparent plot
news to be published
there was a *New York Times* edition to get out
how the sun set on the *New York Times* building
and after setting in brilliant gold
became a human head
and that after moments turned into cartoon figures
a comic strip in the air
a punchline after all
animals in cartoon scenes
there was the human story there
there was the larger purpose becoming visible

for the breakfast of the New Age
was being prepared

it wasn't the expected turn
the return of Robert

as Ulysses this time
to tell the story of
why death was being dislodged
he had seen it
the second hand now seen for what it was
Man was getting the story secondhand

living a version that was secondhand
but a revision had been sent
the manuscript as it really was
the script for Man
the blueprint
the Uman script

and not the secondhand
but first-
hand

He had gotten the thread
the thread that tied up the past
this was not the Old Man
was a totally New Man
the missing link

For the cancer had only been for purpose of re-
mission
this death and many other deaths
something tremendous was in the air
as the past became clarified
Man at a rhet-
Turn
a revelation under way
a modern Gospel
the prophetic line of humanity
reaching the point of its leap of faith

The whole human race taking a leap together?
Yes, the whole human race
leaping out of
the end of the world
finding there was an alternative to the
end of the world

There was a new plan.

II

But how is it possible that Life was extradited
right under man's nose
and we didn't do a thing
took our own life away
and we didn't do a thing
for knowing nothing about it
knew nothing at all about this practice of X-
Tradition

In springtime
Man in springtime
given
A blue-
Print
the trump
ET

Mozart his last SPRING
springTIME
in
E-
té[10]

For we have two Christs here
one who stopped
and one would join him
in
E-
té

You've never played with me
Com-
Plet[11]

---

[10] *été*–summer; pronounced "a-tay"; rhymes with "Dan-te" and roughly "*complet.*" Mozart wrote "Longing for Springtime" (1791) just before his birthday; he died December 5; word play in *The Christ State* includes *printemps*–spring (FR); *temps*–time, as in Print Time

[11] *complet*–complete (FR); pronounced. "comb play"

End of the world
suddenly what do we see
Pier-
O[12]

---

[12] Pierrot—pron "pier row," a clown

III

The call to Man had come
The telephone rang
It was Christ on the line

rounding up followers
asking who was with him.
Which of us would make this jump into the
twenty-first century
the telephone to the earth rang
it was Christ calling

A young man has the preparation ready

In celebration
in jubilation
Co-may-
Dia

A view of the world
from a high perspective
Come-
Dia

In 1492 the Genoese
Cristóbal Colón
set sail from Spain
looking for a shortcut to the East
to make a trade route to the East
the land of spices
set said looking for the connection
some link, some opening
to shorten the distance
a direct route
some body of water

found, though
two continents full of gold
even hanging from Native Americans' noses

Began the Colonial period
when it was really something in Man
meant to be COLONized
given the
equality symbol

The breakthrough
passageway
arrived at indirectly
he sought
directly
geographically
between East and West
de-
colonization
of the inner Man

A Good SHOW

And God said
this should make a
Good
chaud[13]

The Home Plot
the Fire Side
out of the
Shad-dough

chaud
French "hot"
fireside
hearth
of the
Light
energy

---

[13] *chaud*—hot (FR), pronounced "show"

The *FOUR*
—where the cooking went on
the radiation went forth—
time reached
the *cook*-key

Dot dot Dash dot dash dash dash
Morse code into my ears, my
unconscious ears,
taking us into the
next century

Come in, Earth
This is Crew
see El
ciel[14]

deeply believing that the Earth is ready for such an
opportunity
Singing into the atmosphere

SAVE
THIS PLANET
the mountain of commitment
this is it

THAT MOUNTAIN

For a truth
from origins beyond the Earth
that until now had not been able
to
now has
Ulysses' love had

---

[14] *ciel*—sky (FR); pron. "see L"; El—God (Hebrew, Phoenician,
etc.); often at the end of prophets' names, as in Ezekiel; "ah" is
similar

PENNY-
TRATED

RUMI-NATIONS

Cells and the Soul

Kill the cell
Consciousness
Moves to another
Cell—
Or no cell
No mind

Oh, but I feel alone
(the personality)
how could *you* be so brave?
Risking me?
(My personality
—to the soul)
—brazen of you to think I could be so courageous

Where did you voyage from, my soul?
Before you were me—
Just
Consciousness
Perhaps of someone else?!
Became me
Quantizing
Consciousness
It's why I feel scared sometimes
Imagining myself as
Quantized

Consciousness

But it's fun, it's fun,
Said the soul
Follow me
And so I took my first out-of-body trip, following
her, to I never found out where,
the
Little Ball of
Quantized
Love
Quantized
Wisdom
Quantized
Into Me

CONCLUSION

Breathing into my belly

It sends ideas up to me
in awareness in the midst of
what's going on
KNOWING
what's going on

—holding
what's going on
—refocusing
sending ideas out
Refocus out

into/to be fashioned into
what's going on
sitting heavily
no desire to move
no need to
aware of
what's
going on

from whence comes this knowledge
mysteriously from nowhere
a Presence
no tracks
how it got there
no word
no indication
in the
Buddha
Belly

the universe
connects with us
so many secrets it has
How

"Drop it"
My light body teacher says

What? It's transpersonal

Yes, but old
Drop it,
My light body teacher says.

Cut off all the past?

Assimilate it, my light body teacher says

Assimilate that old Eastern teaching
Hindu and Buddhist
From centuries
In the
Buddha belly
Look to what's coming in
Drop that ancient wisdom

Just cut it off?

No,
Assimilate it

Once my spine was all mixed up
My personality was one place
My consciousness disconnected
I couldn't find it
Duane, my light body co-founder,

When I told him
Touched the vibrational energy body and light body
centers, up the spine
And
a cobra (kundalini) shot out through and
over my head
sitting like lotus petals there
Following the light body path

Cobra learning the light body centers

And so, time rolled around
Again the ancient teaching
And what's next
regrouping and
assimilating

For the first time
In step with the times
Contempo-
rary

Light of step
Not mincing words
Understood
What tempo?
contemporary

I can feel the consciousness as it sits in me
It can sit anywhere
Sits in me, holding the space

No shape?
a big belly
Not to it
it's just aware energy—large, yes, wanting to poke out
Taking up
no space at all in time
Just
THERE

not out of step with the time?
Found the beat at last

stepping out the door into life
into being understood
for you have made me
contempo-
rary

My Hair

I lost my hair
2022

Every strand growing back
is the history of me
Red roots
at the tips gray

Red-headed baby
climbing
to eighty
a single-thread
history

illness took my hair away
supposedly
But, I ask you, was it
 a chance to grow back All of Me?

How far back?

Where did I start?
Infant to
NOW

in
step
stepping
UP

Con-
Tempo
rary

PART
FIVE

You predicted you?
Yes, I predicted me. And then again—the signs were
always there. A signpost here, a signpost there, at all
the turns in the road.
I followed a
trail
To Me
lifting off from the "wrong future."
I heard my "future" call
but it was not my future self at all
It was "me," fully formed in the potential I had only
to grasp

So here we are in 1996.
Ten/eleven years after the Zurich Initiation
"I" was there then
What did I—the one writing then, in 1985—know
about
multiple dimensions of consciousness
Only that I was in a soul grouping that was spreading
the awareness of the universality of us all
Me, you, us all
But what did that mean?
Even caught right in the midst of its demonstrations
down in 1985/'86 in the Earth, in the room *where I*
was,
I didn't know
I only kept in mind a direct line between myself and
the Zurich

Initiator, whom I was listening to and watching
demonstrate what Eastern gurus called *siddhis* but we
in the West called miracles—"tricks" of energy
mastery we said were not possible
But I believed "him," even when he said that on the
"fourth level" of himself he was the Christ
That was in 1985, 1986
This poem is pieced together from a file in 1996 that
I called
A Mary Magdalene Book
Who was I then?
The one headed toward the me now
if I just followed where I understood and didn't
But felt
I felt my way to here

From a folder titled

To Love—AND Remember

A Mary Magdalene Book—
For all those in
her energy
and there are many

Candles, come
tell us about some
who wanted to help change
the old Earth

Led, entering, into your dreams at night
to wake you up
but you are awake
it would seem
in your universe
but not in mine and so
I tell you so
in your dreams
and then you do in fact
wake
Counterpoint unusual
universe to universe

262Xyou   who are in another
universe

262.
Tentmaking.
Ac. 18:3, 1 Th
2:9

to whom I go in your dreams
I wonder
Do you feel the presence of me
as I gaze at your picture
feel that you love someone
and don't know where to look
for I am in another world
visiting in the nighttime you

that I can now do what you did for me
so many times
so many places
and that it lasts forever
the love that began in eternal flames
and that still is in them
in this universe and the lengths to that other universe
and the crashed landings back into me here

but I didn't care
just so long as I got there
and went into
your dreams

I am told you won't recognize me
when we meet again
or will recognize me
but not know
from when

I go into your dreams
make them vivid and real
in intensity of the journey it took
in overwhelming warmth and sunshine
and a sense of being in the room
so you can recognize when I come there again
and that must somehow stay embedded in the cells
like an instinct
An instinctive recognition of the meaning of that
presence
and that it loves you
and then what love must be
For you know it's not in your world

It would violate your purpose if you came to me now
but it must help to know
you are important to someone
there are things about you
you don't know

A telescope that let me see changing-shaped stars
the day I dreamed you returned
to another planet
and told them about me
that the planet shapes—in the sky—shifted and made
kaleidoscopic forms
that we on the ground
all saw, though it must have been some kind of
illusion
you made

that I now, in the changing roles
show you things you could never imagine
which were all the ways you taught me
all the things I knew nothing of
until you
showed me

O, Personalities, who think your lives short and
ended,
you go on in us, the soul
you go on and on in memory
and how barren and at a loss it would be
a soul without such
personality memories
such as those made
between you
and
me

that the deprivation we experienced
did not merely die unmourned

that it was not for nothing
not a grave without flowers on it
every single day

Not weeds, not a single one of them
not overgrown and broken, abandoned adornments
not overturned pots
not any of this on the grave of us
For we left no stone unturned
once out of physical confinement
the heart burst the bonds and ropes
once the magnitude of the feeling was sensed
once the boat adrift
Reached its moorings
once the knowledge did penetrate
and sweep away
All of the knowledge

of what life is
what is possible
none of it mattered
not beside
this knowledge

O, heart, why did you stay closed so long
Why did you sense danger
which was there
it is there
but that does not weigh against this knowledge
stronger as light is
came to show the showers of joy it could have
brought
and so did bring in
another
way
you made me Penelope and left
you, Ulysses, do not know who it is who is waiting

and where she waits and will join you
someday

Is it possible?
It is just a trick of the mind to think
any other
way

If experience is stronger than knowledge
than the prove-ale
—if it intersects and counteracts
even countersends
laws of fact
—then what is this?
Isn't *what is* what is experienced and remains
in the soul's library
in the eternal vault
in time's treasure chest
in our and my picture album?

and neither life nor death
nor anything in heaven and earth
can change that
isn't that the meaning
of eternity?

—eternity that can sit on a toadstool
be a leprechaun
wink
lift us into a suspended experience
animation that doesn't breathe or move
isn't all that eternity's form
isn't it the reason I know this?

Intangibility
become tangible
that if you were X square then my form would be too
the X
square
that is
you

our energy form
when it has a form
not merely presence
of me feeling the nearness

as the Initiator, the cosmic being in Zurich
you told me on your fourth level
you were Jesus
manifestation and essence, what's the difference
past and present
nowness
of the soul's
experience

You were
a service he wanted to give
a form reformed originally
for no one could be more original
thought I
And yet this is only part of
and an experience of
the wholeness of that
totally ORIGINAL
incarnate
Christness

You were my experience of love
my seed of the Christ
what I knew of such things
until you came
holding them like mana
not saying
what they were

Divine grace
Divine love
names

Xungiven

unspecified
for words

were   sparse and counted

Count each word
how many?
loved in the speaking
put into position
to be recorded
just as
from
Jesus

I your memory container
who go into your dreams
to

Xkeep   warm and renewed

this strange encounter that
centuries apart now
and eons in time
still finds a path

to meet through

and who dare walk into it

walk, crawl through them
the corridors
of Unlocked Time

time, in its mighty crescendos
what wave is this you transported
the door of the opening of the heart of the century

who was it that died in that dark corridor?
the idea

that afterdeath was a state of destruction
it was but of the
being stuck
and not of the good that remained
the good luck
unresisted
walked into
in that unlocked cylinder where there waited
the One awaited
MET

The unspent resources of faith
in its cathedral
the unending windingness of the answers leading to
the spot where
they arise
A need for it
Brought in
Justlikethat
Now connecting to *then*

What will block our steps
Separate us from
Our e-
mergence

All through my back the connections ran
at every vertebra hid one
all through my past these openings into this century
the Heraclites positions of myself
could that be?
Could there be so many connections
in my own rememberings
of myself
and you
or then of this century and its planned openings into
the new opportunities

its openings into eternity
how many points
were touched

how many bruises taken away
many bandages removed
how many blinders stepped out behind from
time and its blinders
in this mighty
crescendo

A wave burst a billowing
there we are on the sail unfurling
Sail on
Time through the gates of
Eternity

Earth time on eternal time
right through the gates and no stopping point
for Earth dreams if you do this

remember your contact points with
your
eternities

And what about Mary Magdalene?
the Mother
on her fourth level

Invisible, unannounced meetings
Unnamed encounters
Loving all of
The forms of you
Anonymously increasing energy
In the third dimension getting a glimpse of itself in
the fourth

Unforgotten the siddhis, going into the consciousness
The Zurich me
Alive in me till
This very day
Making me me
My Square I
The first moment I started to remember
The purpose of this lifetime, unreached without that
encounter
The potential in the waiting room

that is "me"

Afterword Conversation with the late great channel Mariah Martin End of December/start of January 2005/2006

My dachshund Snoepie is dying, having seizures. It's just a matter of time. "He wants to get you into your new house," she says. Hunter S. Thompson has just passed over; I've brought out his letters and sketched a memoir based in them, bringing in my three powerful New York City male "teachers"/boyfriends from the mid-1960s, daring now to go into that period publicly. It's a draft of *Keep This Quiet!*

MAH: it will be "a great shock to people [who know me through my earlier writing] when they see the shift," I tell her. But "my initiation in Zurich was just as extreme."

Mariah says that's OK.

MAH: You gave me the term "the human Christ" for the initiator. Do you have more insight now regarding where I am . . . and how the initiation was conducted? Every aspect of my life has [had] challenges.

MARIAH: Every aspect of life has a birth process . . . Let the walls come tumbling down.

She suggests I do a little ritual before each writing—"remembering that it's an ancestral journey of the soul you're to be now."

I say this soul who came to initiate me in 1985 seemed to be saying he was Jesus, *but not on all levels.*

She says, "It's a consciousness state [the Christ consciousness state], but not the only consciousness [state] in existence.

MAH: I thought it was a particular entity, and that's the problem I'm having. He seemed to be able to be part of anybody, that he had this energy and could withdraw it.

MARIAH answers.

MAH: So basically he had this structure where everybody could put their energy in and out and withdraw it and you point out that "as an entity, you can identify with your nonlocal consciousness. It's not like saying, "This is Jesus, and only he could have been there." So why did they focus on the Jesus and Mary history?

MARIAH: Because you have journeyed through many civilizations and worked through this archetype many times.

MAH: So all I knew at the time was I was a "personality of Mary." And Virginia [my friend who was advising me] will restrict me to that.

MARIAH: It's important to distinguish that you are the consciousness of that being without being that being.

MAH: So the question then becomes, "Does that entity exist?"

MARIAH: That's still a question.

MAH: So, that Mary entity, holding that consciousness at that time, was holding the Mary energy, which comes from the Goddess energy, which had been held many times? But I certainly didn't have a clue then."

MARIAH: People don't.

MAH: Basically, this is showing how I go through this process where you are encountering collective energy, the Universal Mind—how you go through it. It's the process of Ascension, isn't it?

MARIAH: "You will do as I do and greater."

You're "entering your fairy self," she tells me, referring to a specific recent event. I felt a rose between my toes just before calling her.

MARIAH: It's an aspect of the energy that knows how to go, alight, from flower to flower and energy source to energy source and go to where it's needed

And: "Some people work on ascending. And some on descending to ground the light." That I am coming down as I watch other people go up, to look for what I already have.

Postscript

It comes to me,
To you
To anyone at all
The Jesus

Energy

I know it
You know it
You recognize it
When you receive
—encounter
It
Don't let anyone ever tell you otherwise
Remember Peter
And so, yes, many times after this the actual Jesus
Did come
And this was

all
Preparation
A leg
To
Stand
on

And what about Mary Magdalene?
the Mother
on her fourth level?

Invisible, unannounced meetings
Unnamed encounters
Universal
Perhaps coming to you
Anonymously increasing energy
In the third dimension getting a glimpse of itself in
the fourth

Leonardo, *Adoration of the Magi,*
Google Art Project

Notes

[1] "Cosmic Dance," posted Nov. 8, 2012, by yrskbalu, https://yrskbalu.blogspot.com/.

Praise for

Margaret A. Harrell's Poetry

Part Four of the Magdalene poems were previously published in *Particle Piñata Poems*.

BookLife (the indie/small-press arm of *Publishers Weekly*) writes, of *Particle Piñata Poems*:

"Harrell's collection is a cosmic, often esoteric whirlwind which seeks to bring the poet's conception of a spiritual being to life. The style is pointedly erratic, even at times frenzied; consistent verb tenses, syntax, and connotations are flouted, upended, redefined. Yet there is a certain naturalness to the poetic discord, like the winds of a hurricane or flurry of a meteor shower."

"The poetry of Margaret Ann Harrell reads like a Zhuangzi of the 21st century, taking its reader through a spiritual Odyssey, where one can hear the cosmic beat in the rhythm of the word play, the pulse of heartfelt mind-blowing experiences revealing a vast span of messages from beyond. It shows the craftmanship of a female shaman who has the power to catch such a dazzling wild and free roaming content into the nets of poems. Here is a . . . *rite de passage* initiating its reader into multiversal dimensions, bringing meaning to life where few have been looking

171

to find it . . . a unique treat, a gift from those who know how to sow the seed for what really matters on earth."—Chris Van de Velde, Zen novice and "Light Looper," Belgium

"The time of the grandmothers, of the nurturing healing feminine energy has arrived. Patriarchy has sewn destruction long enough. We must all, female and male, become healers, seers. In her epic PARTICLE PINATA, author Margaret Ann Harrell stands in direct lineage with the desert mystics, the poet prophets of old and, simultaneously, with the contemporary cutting edge avant-garde. In a whirling dance with the creative forces of the universe Harrell draws explicit and implicit lines to Rumi, Blake, Yeats, Joyce, Jung, and others while forging mystical connections with clouds and coastlines, dancing in the borderlands of space and time, of being and not being, of embracing and letting go. And she accomplishes it all in her own distinctly original poetic voice. Through decades of carrying these poems from continent to continent, Margaret Ann Harrell has continued to add new poems and photos, to edit and revise, to transform her self into an ever evolving being, into this masterpiece book. I can't recommend it highly enough. Go ahead, open the front cover and enter. You'll never be the same."—Ron Whitehead, U.S. National Beat Poet Laureate

About the Author

Photo credit: Bill Hardesty

Three-time MacDowell fellow Margaret A Harrell is an author, editor, and experimental cloud photographer exhibited in Europe and the US. Also, an advanced meditation teacher in the DaBen/Orin light body school.

She is the author of the coffee table collectible *The* Hell's Angels *Letters: Hunter S. Thompson, Margaret Harrell and the Making of an American Classic* in conjunction with Ron Whitehead (Norfolk

Press), the *Keep This Quiet!* I–IV memoir series, as well as *Particle Pinata Poems, Cloud Conversations*, and a host of other books. Harrell copy-edited/assistant-edited Hunter S. Thompson's first book, *Hell's Angels.* Currently she mentors those wanting to maximize their potential. Her other audiobooks include *The* Hell's Angels *Letters, An Underground PRINCIPIA, and Stop All the Clocks.* For many years, she lived outside the United States, in Morocco, Switzerland (studying at the C. G. Jung Institute), and Belgium. Academically, she has an MA in literature from Columbia University and a BA in history from Duke. A sought-after speaker, she is often on panels, including at the Gonzofest in Louisville, Kentucky and New Orleans—currently in charge of some of the panels for the 2026 Gonzo Fest in New York City.

Thank You for Reading My Book

If you enjoyed it, I would deeply appreciate an honest review on Amazon and/or another platform. I will read every word you write and benefit from the comments.

Connect with me on Facebook, Linked In, and through my website, https://margaretharrell.com. Start a discussion with me.

You cannot know how much I appreciate your reading my books.